MW01247050

Farmer Brown And The Birds

Frances Margaret Fox

FARMER BROWN AND
THE BIRDS

BY
FRANCES MARGARET FOX

Illustrated by
ETHELDRED B. BARRY

BOSTON
L. C. PAGE & COMPANY
1900

Colonial Press

Electrotyped and Printed by C. H. Simonds & Co.

Boston, Mass., U. S. A.

" Indeed, it is not too much to say, that without birds the earth would not long be habitable."

—Frank Chapman.

ILLVSTRATIONS

FARMER BROWN AND THE BIRDS.

―――

CHAPTER I.

"Of all the cowardly, sneaking tricks I ever heard of, that's the worst. Really, madam, you ought not to stand it."

"But what can I do?" protested the Brown Turkey, dismally. "Again and again I have followed Farmer Brown about, begging him to help me. I have told him that I have a nest in the grass by the fence, and that there is nothing I want so much in this world as a brood of little turkeys, but that every day, when I lay an egg, a miserable old Crow steals it the minute I leave the nest."

"Madam, it is a burning shame! Doesn't Farmer Brown notice you at all?"

"Oh, yes," sighed the Turkey, "but I am quite out of patience with him ; he only laughs a little and gives me something to eat. As if that did any good! Something to eat, indeed, when your heart is broken!"

The Wren hopped nervously about, uncertain what to say. He felt so sorry for his good-natured door-yard friend, — the poor Brown Turkey.

"Ah, madam," said he, "if my wife Jennie could see that Crow! She isn't afraid of anybody — Jennie isn't — and, oh, how she can scold! If the cat happens to come near our house, she sputters so fast and so loud that some one is sure to come out and drive it away. She's a great fighter, is my wife Jennie. Why, pardon me, Mrs. Turkey, of course, none of us are to blame if we are not born fighters, but if my wife Jennie was half your size, I believe she would eat that Crow!"

"Ha — ha — ha — caw — caw — caw! I wouldn't taste half so good as Turkeys' eggs, tell your Jennie," said Jim Crow, coming from his hiding-place near by, and perching on the fence.

"So you've been talking to the farmer about

me, have you?" he laughingly continued. "I
didn't know that you cared to keep your eggs.
Why didn't you say so? I thought you laid
them on purpose for me. Ha — ha — ha —
caw — caw — caw!"

"Madam," said the Wren, shaking with anger,
"it may be useless for a gentleman to speak to
such an insulting rascal, but I am going to give
him a piece of my mind, and as the feathers
may fly before I say all I intend to, I would
rather you wouldn't stay here."

The Brown Turkey had no thought of de-
serting her champion, however, and coura-
geously followed him to the fence. "If my
wife Jennie could only see me now," he called
to her, as he savagely ruffled his feathers.

The dauntless little fellow was in the midst
of a most cutting speech, which made Jim Crow
roar with laughter, when Farmer Brown came
out and saw Jim Crow, in his elegant suit of
black, perched on the corn-field fence.

"The cunning rascal," he commented, and
growing indignant, he retraced his steps to the
house, returning with a gun.

The Crow knew better than to trifle longer,
and to his credit be it said that he warned the

little Wren of danger. Another moment, and the loud report of the gun awoke the echoes, and startled the drowsy cattle near.

High over head sailed the Crow, safe and unhurt, uttering protest after protest in true Crow fashion, while in the deep grass by the roadside lay a motionless Wren — shot by Farmer Brown.

Who would miss one little Wren in a world so full of birds ?

In a small wooden house on top of a pole was a nest, — a home. The makers of the nest had carefully piled a heap of grass and sticks before the entrance of the house, that no one might peep at the treasures within.

A family — six baby birds and a mother — lived in the nest, and they mourned for the Wren shot by Farmer Brown.

Down by the road where the dead Wren lay, an excited group of birds were talking.

"Something ought to be done!" exclaimed the Catbird, puffing his feathers out in a pompous manner. "One of the noblest Wrens on the farm, — an old resident, — the father of a helpless family, has been killed! Let us find the offender and punish him!"

"My friends," said an English Sparrow, "I believe that the little Wren was killed by a cruel boy. In the city from which I came, my family suffer an endless persecution. Tiny and harmless as I am, there is a price upon my head. We Sparrows are called the tramps of the bird world, and our lives are always in danger. Yet are we not tramps, but soldiers, and we belong in the cities, where we can conquer the foes of man. Don't be impatient, for I am in earnest. I mean that from daylight till dark we work, picking up every bit of decaying matter we can find that would poison the air, if left in the street. We are always fighting — "

"No doubt about it," ventured a Blue Jay.

"Ah, my friends," continued the Sparrow, earnestly, "the time has come for us to unite and teach men and boys not to kill the birds."

"Sparrow," questioned a Meadow-lark, "we

are but simple birds of the orchard and fields. If we are unjustly treated, what can we do? What shall we do?   Sparrow, you are city bred: tell us how men redress their wrongs?"

"Men have courts of justice where the inno-cent and guilty tell their stories before wise judges who punish crime and wrong-doing," replied the Sparrow.

"Are not our Owls wise as the judges of men?" eagerly suggested a Chickadee, "and may we not hold court and redress our own wrongs?"

"Why not?" asked a Phœbe-bird, and "Why not?" echoed all the gathering.

"Good!" said the Sparrow.   "The first thing to be done is to call a coroner's jury and hold an inquest."

"For years I lived beneath the eaves of the city hall," announced a Barn Swallow, "so let me be the coroner, and the Robin, Brown Thrush, Meadow-lark, Bluebird, Bobolink, and Oriole shall be my jury."

In a few moments the jury solemnly declared, as their verdict, that the Wren's death was caused by a shot from a gun in the hands of a person unknown to them.

There is a little feathered fellow known as the "Preacher Bird," who has a habit of saying, "You see it? You know it? Do you hear me? Do you believe it?" He is the Red-eyed Vireo; and just at twilight, so it is said, hearing the Thrushes sadly singing by the quiet form of the Wren, he thought it his duty to join them and preach the funeral sermon.

While the Mourning Doves sang a plaintive chant, the Robins covered their little comrade with leaves, and the Burying Beetles lowered him into the grave.

Then all the birds went home, and the chirping of the Crickets was the only sound by the roadside, when the night and the stars looked down upon the earth.

CHAPTER II.

FAR and near went the news of the death and burial of the Wren, and one day Jim Crow, who was away from home examining corn-fields in regard to future prospects, learned of the interest the birds were taking, and the curiosity as to who killed the little Wren.

"Man's inhumanity ought to be brought before our communities," thought the Crow, slowly shaking his black head, and acting as innocent as though he had never stolen Turkeys' eggs; "we do our best, season after season, to keep the worms and insects in check, and what is our reward? Why even the Robins risk their lives if they but taste of the cherries they have worked for. The first thing these farmers know, there won't be a bird left, and what sort of crops will they have then? A pretty world this would be without birds! That poor little Wren is dead, but it isn't too late to warn the

18

rest of my friends to look out for guns. Anyway," he added, "there is no use in staying near
this field, for the corn tastes like tar, — I really
believe it was soaked in tar before it was planted.
Bah! what Crow would eat such stuff as this?"

When Jim Crow reached home, the first bird
he met was his cousin, who asked him if he had
heard the news about the Wren.

"Certainly," answered Jim, proceeding to tell
an astonishing story of his own, although often
interrupted by the loud "caws" of his impatient
listener.

"Now let me tell you what the birds have
done!" chimed in his cousin. "You see, that
little city Sparrow told us all about how men
hold court. The ways men have of righting
wrongs are so remarkably wise that only a few
of the men themselves can understand about it,
so they have lawyers who spend their whole
lives in learning about the law, and these lawyers
help the poor men in the courts. Now, as you
know, the laws of the birds are very simple — "

"Yes, but what are we going to do with
Farmer Brown?" asked Jim Crow.

"You are as impatient as a hungry nestling,
Jim," laughed the other. "I was going to say

that we birds couldn't decide what to do, as the
little city Sparrow said we couldn't follow the
ways of men exactly, because, in this case,
the wrong was done by a race other than our
own.   Just then a pretty Bluebird suggested
telling the Owls about it and asking their advice.
But no one dared go to the Owls at night,
though we tease the poor things enough in the
daytime, until one of the birds said Sparrow
should go, as he knew better than any of us
what to say.   Sparrow was badly frightened,
but after calling himself a soldier, what could
he do but go?   For a wonder the Owls didn't
eat him up, but listened to his story; then they
held a council, attended by birds of their feather
from far and near.

"The council of the Owls decided that the
Wren was killed by a man or boy, for, as they
reasoned, who else could fire a gun?   To find
that man or boy is the important thing; having
found him, to give him a trial to prove his inno-
cence or guilt.   The Sparrow insists that in
America, where we live, a man accused of
wrong-doing is supposed to be innocent until
his guilt is sure.   The council, with the advice of the Sparrow, appointed the officers

"THE OWLS . . . LISTENED TO HIS STORY."

necessary for the trial, and sent a message to each.   They chose a Long-eared Owl for justice of the peace, and a Hawk Owl, representing the only species of day Owls, for Judge of the Great Court.   Five other Owls are to act as a Supreme Court, if we need one.

" Now, Jim, the thing for you to do is to go to the justice of the peace and tell your story — "

" Why didn't you tell me that long ago ? " exclaimed Jim Crow, restlessly flapping his wings.

" But," protested his cousin, " I haven't told you all there is."

" Well, you have told me enough for the present, so let us call on his Honour, the justice."

Straightway to the Long-eared Owl went the two friends, and solemnly declared that Farmer Brown killed the Wren.

" Who ? Who ? Who ? " nervously asked the judge.   Then, as if too surprised for further speech, he listened quietly while Jim Crow told his story.   " What ought we to do now ? " said he, in a helpless way, to the English Sparrow, who had flown to his side when Jim Crow appeared.

"Send for the sheriff, — you remember Raven is sheriff. Tell him to keep his eye on the farmer, to watch all he does, and to inform him that he is the prisoner of the birds."

In the dead of the night the birds on the farm were awakened by a hoarse voice calling, "Who killed the Wren? Who? Who? Who? Come to the court of the Long-eared Owl and you may know who — who — who!"

At daybreak the grove in which the Long-eared Owl chose to hold court was alive with curious birds who obeyed the midnight summons.

"Fellow citizens," said the justice, and instantly the twittering and chirping ceased, "Farmer Brown is charged with the murder of the Wren. He is now our prisoner. The Sparrow Hawk, appointed by our council to be his attorney, says he wishes to enter a plea of 'Not guilty' for the farmer. As it will soon be so light that I cannot see, even in this dim shade, I hope the Blue Jay, who is attorney for the Feathered Tribe, will examine the witnesses as quickly as possible."

Thereupon, the bird in blue and the bird in black took their places, each giving himself many an important air as he did so.

"What is your name?" asked the Blue Jay, gravely.

"James Crow!" was the answer.

"How old are you?"

"That I don't know."

"Are you married or single?" continued the Blue Jay, who had been told by the English Sparrow from the city to ask these questions.

"I am married," said the Crow, with a great show of dignity.

"Where do you live?"

"Tenth story, tree number 15, Pine Grove Avenue," answered the Crow, wondering when he would have a chance to tell what he wanted to about Farmer Brown.

"What is your occupation?"

"State Food Inspector."

"What do you know about the death of the Wren?"

The Crow's face brightened as the birds crowded nearer, for was he not popular among them at last?

"One day, when the apple-trees were in full bloom, neighbour Wren and I were perched on the corn-field fence having a visit, when Farmer Brown came out with a gun in his hand. I always fly when I see a gun, and I warned the Wren to follow; but he was such a friendly, unsuspecting little fellow, he wouldn't do it; he even scolded me in lively style for being a coward. Almost instantly I heard the report of the gun and saw neighbour Wren fall to the ground — dead — as I well knew."

"That is enough," said the Blue Jay. "We thank you for your evidence, and will now hear what our friend in the white vest and gray coat has to say."

With stately grace the King-bird came forward. "Sir," said he, slowly, "I am ever so old, and my business is Inspector of Beehives. I am well acquainted with Mr. Brown, who has more than once tried to shoot me when he has found me ridding the beehives of drones and

robber flies. No wonder the Wren wasn't afraid
of him. He knew he couldn't shoot straight,
for we have often talked about it. Jim Crow
must be easily frightened if he was afraid of
Farmer Brown with a gun in his hand, — why,
that man couldn't hit the side of a barn if he
tried to."

"Come, come," said the Owl, severely, "you
mustn't laugh in court."

"Did you see Farmer Brown kill the Wren?"
questioned the Blue Jay.

"Yes, I did, though I am sure he hit him by
accident. It is just as Jim said; he and the
Wren were on the fence when the farmer came
with his gun; he must have aimed at Jim or at
a Turkey in the grass, for when he fired, the
shot struck the Wren."

"How did you happen to be there?" persisted the Jay.

"Was just resting after a fight with a Purple
Martin." While the birds were laughing at the
further explanations of the King-bird, the Owl
devoured several fat mice he had provided for
a lunch.

Jim Crow's eyes grew round with wonder when
the Song Sparrow was called as a third witness.

"My home," said he, "is Dry Grass Cottage on Meadow Path, — such a tiny, pleasant home. Of course you all know I belong to a concert company. One summer day, when the grass-hoppers were young and tender, I was perched on a tree near the fence upon which the Crow and the Wren were talking, when I saw Farmer Brown shoot the Wren. Just as soon as my babies can fly," concluded the Song Sparrow, earnestly, "we will leave this farm for ever; we won't trust ourselves near a man who shoots his best friends."

"You don't need to listen to more evidence," whispered the English Sparrow to the sleepy Owl, who was winking and blinking in a very stupid fashion, while the jolly old sun shone brighter and brighter as if to tease him. "The farmer ought to be put in jail until the Hawk Owl is ready to call his case; as it is, perhaps the Raven better tell him that he is held for trial before our higher tribunal."

"Court is adjourned!" announced Justice Owl, and away went the birds, calling out and scolding in so lively a style that Farmer Brown, on his way to milk the cows, wondered what the trouble could be.

CHAPTER III.

In an open meadow, where the sunshine loved to linger, came flocks of birds to attend the trial of Farmer Brown. On a flat stone sat the solemn-faced judge, grave and silent in the midst of the light-hearted, merry throng, with their restless, fluttering wings.

At the appointed hour, the stately Raven by his side called out in mournful tones: "Hear ye, hear ye, hear ye! The Great Court of the Feathered Tribe is now in session. All birds who have been unjustly treated by mankind, draw near and you shall be heard."

"Who sins against the birds, sins against man's best friends," announced the judge. During the hush that followed, the Blue Jay briefly told the story of the death of the Wren, and the many reasons for believing that Farmer Brown killed him.

"What do you plead?" said the judge, turn-

ing to the bird who was to defend the farmer;
"guilty or not guilty?"

"Not guilty," quickly answered the Sparrow
Hawk, believing Farmer Brown would have
said the same thing; for, suppose he killed the
Wren, would he think that a serious matter?
Would he consider himself guilty of murder?

There was a lively time in the meadow court
when the jury was chosen. The Butcher-bird
wanted to be a juror, but when he said he
would hang the farmer the Sparrow Hawk
frowned; and when a pure white Dove said
he loved the farmer, the Blue Jay laughingly
advised him to sit beside the Butcher-bird and
have a visit with him, as neither of them could
act as jurors.

Twelve of the common birds on the farm
were finally chosen to try the case of Farmer
Brown. Among them was a Wren, who, in the
happy days gone by, had played many a game
of "tag" with the unfortunate little mother
Wren who now found herself the centre of so
much attention; he made up his mind that, if he
could do anything to help her, he would.

The Meadow-larks ate grasshoppers and the
Wood-pewees and Phœbe-birds ate flies all the

" ' NOT GUILTY,' QUICKLY ANSWERED THE SPARROW HAWK. "

time, while the Cuckoos devoured caterpillars as long as there were any to be found,
and then left the court for more. The judge
enviously watched the Hawks eat mice.

Even the Blue Jay looked surprised at the
hungry multitude, as he rose to address the
judge and jury :

"Your Honour, birds of the jury," said he, in
his most pleasing manner, "this is the case
of the Feathered Tribe against Farmer Brown.
We, the birds of the farm, expect to prove that
Farmer Brown killed the Wren. We also intend
to prove that the cruel deed was done without
cause, that there was no reason whatever for
the act, and from the jury we shall expect a
verdict of guilty against the farmer, who must
then be punished for his crime, that we may
teach mankind to value the lives of birds."

After Jim Crow, who was careful not to
mention Turkeys, the King-bird, and Song Sparrow had again given their testimony, the Blue
Jay called the Baltimore Oriole as a witness.

"My home," said he, "is Swinging Cradle
Cottage, Branch Street, near the corn-field. I
have known Farmer Brown ever since he was
a nestling and have always liked him, — such a

kind, good man he is. I was well acquainted
with the Wren, too; he was a good neighbour
and a great help to the farmer, as he destroyed
bugs by the thousand. One day, when I was
sitting near my home watching my mate weave
a bit of grass about the door, I noticed Jim
Crow and the Wren on the fence below me.
Just when I was wondering what they, with
their different tastes and habits, could find to
talk about, the farmer came out with a gun in
his hand. I saw him take aim, fire, and kill the
Wren. Wasn't I surprised! The noise the gun
made frightened my babies so that, if they
hadn't been in a deep nest, I believe they would
have fallen out. How I wish all you birds
would learn to make hanging nests, they are so
much safer, and — "

"Let us now hear what the Meadow-lark has
to say," interrupted the Blue Jay. "Where do
you live, friend Meadow-lark, and what is your
business?"

"They call me a professor of entomology,
Mr. Jay, and my home is Arched Cottage, on
Grass Lane. In that little home I have six
children who are always crying for food. Like
us, they prefer grasshoppers and the choicest

insect dainties. One day, when I had found some plump bugs and beetles which I was carrying home for my clamouring youngsters, I saw Farmer Brown shoot the Wren. Now, I know that Farmer Brown has often tried to kill Hawks and Crows, but, if I hadn't seen him do it, I wouldn't have believed that he would shoot one of his own folks, as you might say."

The Blue Jay's last witness was the mother Wren, who came into court with her eight children. Before her story was half told the little things began opening their mouths and begging for food, so the birds were very glad when court adjourned and they could offer the babies a feast. How the mother bird laughed when she saw the Robins bringing great earthworms for her family; she supposed that every one knew that Wrens live only on tiny worms, bugs, and flies.

Soon after sunrise the following morning the birds again met in the meadow to listen to the testimony of the farmer's friends.

"Your Honour, birds of the jury," said the Sparrow Hawk, "we admit that Farmer Brown killed the Wren, but at the same time we claim and will prove that he was quite innocent of evil intent, and that he shot the Wren by accident. Friend Swallow, kindly tell us what you know about Farmer Brown?"

In a musical voice, low and pleasing, a Barn Swallow addressed the birds:

"Farmer Brown's barn has been my home as long as I can remember. From early morning until late at night, through many a long summer, I have seen him coming and going about his work, and I have never known him to do an unkind act. If he killed the Wren, and knows it, his punishment must be enough already, for he would sorrowfully think of his deed many times a day. Farmer Brown cannot shoot straight, and that alone proves that he didn't intend to shoot the Wren, and it is unreasonable to suppose that he did. None of our family ever dreamed that he would harm a bird. On rainy mornings we had often talked with our friends, the Martins, about what a kind man he is. He says we are a real blessing to his horses and cows because we catch the flies in the barn yard. A man cruel enough to kill an innocent little bird, intentionally, wouldn't care whether the flies tormented his horses or not. He is a guiltless man, and deserves all the help we can give him."

When the Barn Swallow was through speaking, a Robin began to talk without waiting to be called. "Don't I know," he protested, "what a noble, kind-hearted man is accused of murder in this court? This spring, with a number of friends, I came north too early, and but for the farmer and his family we should have starved to death. They fed us with crumbs from their own table, and let us eat with the chickens, besides. The children were taught to respect our rights, and we have always been treated with kindness."

"Not so fast," interrupted the Blue Jay; "didn't the farmer ever act out of patience with you in cherry season?"

"Oh, yes," slowly admitted the witness, "he often called us 'pesky Robins.'"

A Quail, who gave his name as Bob White, said that he once met Farmer Brown in the woods with a gun in his hands. "You can't guess how frightened I was," continued the Quail, "but the farmer only said, 'I would never kill so thin a bird as you, Bob White. Why, you'd scarcely make shadow soup.' Now, I think that if the farmer liked to kill birds, he would have been more apt to kill me than a Wren. Farmer Brown really doesn't seem to know how useful we are on the farm."

There was silence in the meadow court when the Chimney Swallow's name was called. He is a bird of curious habits, and never is known to associate with his feathered neighbours. It was very hard for the Sparrow Hawk to question him, for he refused to alight anywhere, flying about as he talked.

"I live in the farmhouse chimney," said he. "I have known Farmer Brown for years. I never lived in the chimney of a better man. One day, not long ago, Mr. Brown came up on the roof to repair it. Our nest is made of twigs glued together and fastened to the inside of the chimney, and my mate and I were dreadfully frightened lest it should be destroyed, with our

four white eggs in it. I told her to keep per-
fectly quiet; that's a thing she can't do, so she
kept up such a clatter that the farmer on the
roof came over and looked in the chimney. My
mate and I both clung to the side of the chimney, supporting ourselves with our claws and
tails, and expecting every minute to be killed.
The farmer told us he wouldn't charge us any
rent, but advised us to feed our young in the
daytime, instead of at night. We never dreamed
of disturbing any one, but Mr. Brown says when
we run up and down the chimney at night, the
noise we make sounds like thunder. The fact
is, we have raised several families and always
fed them at night. Any Chimney Swallow will
tell you that is the best time to feed young
birds. My mate and I both think Mr. Brown a
most patient, considerate man; neither of us
think he killed the Wren."

A Downy Woodpecker was then called to the
witness-stand, but, instead of saying anything in
favour of the farmer, he made all the birds
laugh by telling why the farmer ought to value
his services.

" You see," said he, "one of these wood-borers
our folks are always after might destroy an en-

tire tree. Then think of the grasshoppers' eggs
we eat, and the May-beetles, plant-lice, ants,
and —"

"Never mind all that," begged the Sparrow
Hawk, "tell us what you know of the ways of
Farmer Brown, — does he kill birds?"

"No, he does not. I have often heard him
tell the boys not to harm us, though that's no
wonder. They couldn't rob our nests anyway,
because we're the smallest woodpeckers there
are, and when we bore a hole in a tree we make
the entrance just large enough to admit —"

"Never mind how you make your nest,"
grumbled the judge, "you are wasting time."

A tiny Yellow Bird and his mate expressed
great faith in the farmer's kind intentions, saying that for several years he had been in the
habit of planting sunflowers that they might eat
the seeds they were so fond of; they even believed that he cultivated thistles for their
special use, and told the jury that thistle
seeds are dainty morsels of food.

An Orchard Oriole, a refined, well-dressed
bird, gave an impressive account of the farmer's
uniform kindness to the orchard birds, who, if
they sometimes helped themselves to fruit, paid

him well by eating the spiders and insects
which would have done great damage if left to
live and multiply.

A gentle Dove from the barn, glancing re-
proachfully at the Crows, said that Farmer
Brown had never been unkind to horses, cows,

dogs, or even cats, and how could any one suppose he would kill a bird.

"Merciful judge," entreated the Dove, turning appealing eyes upon the staring Owl, "do not condemn an innocent man, whose actions we, the simple birds, fed by his bounty, have no right to question. He is greater than mere birds. This court has a right to punish one of the feathered race for a wrong committed, but there is no justice in what we do if —"

"Put him in jail," roared the judge. The Raven sheriff immediately approached the surprised Dove, and conducted him to the deserted nest of a Woodpecker, where he kept him imprisoned for two long hours.

The last witness for the defence of the farmer was a pretty Chickadee, who testified that he once heard Farmer Brown say that Wrens were of great use in the garden, and that he especially mentioned the dead Wren as an old friend, worth his weight in gold, whom he was glad to welcome back each spring.

CHAPTER IV.

THE third day of the trial of Farmer Brown was very warm. The Hawk Owl drooped his wings in a listless manner, slowly opened and shut his eyes, and appeared weary of his rôle of judge.

Notwithstanding the weather, however, the usual number of birds appeared in the meadow whose feathers were yet damp from recent baths and who unceremoniously made their toilets in public. The Blue Jay was as wide awake as the Hawk Owl was sleepy. He well knew that Farmer Brown was a favourite with the majority of the birds, and had sought far and wide for more witnesses against him. "Not so much because I want the farmer punished," said the rogue to himself, "but because of my pride as a Blue Jay. How could I endure being defeated by a Sparrow Hawk? A Sparrow Hawk, indeed! Not while my feathers are blue shall one of that tribe conquer me!"

43

Even the judge stared in wonder when the Blue Jay called his first witness, and few of the birds knew whether to laugh or be solemn when the dignified Crane appeared among them.

"My friends and neighbours," said he, "although I am not personally acquainted with many of you, and have always been a bird of retiring habits, yet our wrongs are the same, our interests are one, and together we must teach men that to sin against the birds is to injure all mankind.

"Now I will tell my story. Long ago I had a mate. She was dear to me, and we were happy together. Year after year, with others of our tribe, we faithfully served Farmer Brown. We were especially useful to him in destroying the black snakes which infested the marsh. Instead of receiving any thanks for our helpfulness, we have ever been relentlessly persecuted. One day when I was returning from the bay shore, I saw Farmer Brown shoot my mate. I saw him carry her bleeding body away by the feet, heard him tell a neighbour that he meant to stuff her, — my beautiful mate, — and," sadly declared the Crane, "she was stuffed, and many a time have I gone to the parlour window at the

"FOR YEARS AND YEARS HE AND HIS TRIBE HAD
FOLLOWED THE FARMER'S PLOUGH."

risk of my life, to see her standing there in the corner, when she ought to be alive and with her family."

As the Crane stalked away across the fields, the Blue Jay cast a triumphant glance at the Sparrow Hawk, who ruffled his feathers and looked anxiously into the faces of the jurors.

The Crow Blackbird said that for years and years he and his tribe had followed the farmer's plough, eating armies of grubs; that beetles, grass-hoppers, crickets, caterpillars, ants, flies, bugs, and spiders were disposed of by himself and neighbours in great quantities. Yet the farmer had treated them with great cruelty and had several times tried to kill them all.

When the Crow Blackbird left the witness-stand, instead of hopping, like the majority of birds, he walked as sedately as Jim Crow, which greatly amused the audience.

The Sandpiper testified that his four children had been stolen by a boy visiting the farm.

"Friend Jay," said a strange voice, "you have not asked for my testimony, but will you let me say a word?"

The Blue Jay, glancing in great surprise at

the speaker, a tall, thin Bittern, gave his consent.

"Farmer Brown was never anywhere near me but once," said he, "and then he came upon me suddenly in the marsh. Sooner than fly, I stood right still with my head up, thinking he would take me for a reed. My heart almost stopped beating, though, when he said, 'Oh, if I had a kodak here I would try a shot at that queer bird.'"

How the jolly Bobolinks laughed at the Bittern's mistake.

The Catbird complained that Farmer Brown allowed his boys to torment and mock the Cat-birds; a Butcher-bird declared his life to be always in danger while he stayed on the farm, and the Cherry-bird protested against what he called the stinginess of the farmer in wanting all the cherries. One of the Humming-birds said that she once saw Mrs. Brown going to church with four dead Humming-birds on her hat, and if the farmer didn't kill them for her, where did she get them?

After a short recess the birds again assembled to hear the arguments of the Blue Jay and the Sparrow Hawk.

"May it please the Court, and birds of the jury," began the Blue Jay, and instantly all the fluttering wings were still. "Although we as a nation have uncomplainingly submitted to the cruelties of man during a long period stained with the blood of our ancestors, yet the time has come when justice must be meted out to the destroyer, when man must enter our courts and answer for his crimes.

"It is well known in our communities that, by hundreds and thousands, our best, noblest, and handsomest citizens have been cruelly slain that their dead bodies might adorn the hats of the women of the land. Yet we have made no protest, no effort to defend ourselves and our help-less families, but have sung our sweetest songs even when our hearts were bursting with grief.

"We have laboured faithfully in the fields and gardens, checking the ravages of insects, and doing all in our power to render the earth a paradise for man. We have cheered and com-forted him at all times and in all places. Our songs have been sung to the rich and poor alike. We have done the utmost to please and amuse the children and to brighten their lives.

"And how has man repaid us? Birds of the
jury, when you go to your winter homes, stop in
Florida, call on the little Blue Herons, and ask
them to tell you what has become of the beautiful snowy Egrets who were so abundant in
Florida twenty years ago.   A chorus of
voices will pour forth a tale of shocking cruelty
and horror! They will tell you that man has
pitilessly destroyed all the white, innocent
creatures, and left their nestlings to starve;
and this that the daughters of man might wear
stolen plumes!

"Man has everywhere been our enemy. He
has shot and ensnared our comrades. He
has stolen our eggs, murdered our nestlings, and
ruined our homes. Catbird will tell you of many
of his cousins, the Mocking-birds of the South,
who have been captured by man, — and are
now wearing their lives away in wire prisons in
this north country.

"Birds of the jury, man must be taught to
respect the rights of birds. We must defend
our homes and our helpless little ones. Farmer
Brown has sinned against us, and while there
may be mercy in our dealings with an erring
mortal, yet, let justice be done."

After another short recess the Sparrow Hawk made his plea. So great was the interest, that friends and enemies, forgetting their quarrels, crowded closely together the better to hear what he might say.

"May it please the Court, and birds of the jury," spoke the Sparrow Hawk, in the impressive silence, "it is my honour and privilege to appear before you in behalf of one who is as innocent of the terrible crime of murder, with which he is charged, as the nestlings in the tree-tops. It is indeed unfortunate that Farmer Brown cannot come before this court and speak for himself.

"In the first place, my friends, we are all indebted to Farmer Brown for our homes; we are his tenants; he has not only given us the material wherewith to make our homes, permitted us to remain in undisturbed possession, but he has himself built houses for his special favourites, the Wrens and the Bluebirds. Neither let us overlook the fact that by his bounty our citizens are fed. To him belong, not only the fruit and grain upon the farm, but the insects and worms as well, and to him we owe our grateful thanks for the many feasts we have partaken of in the pleasant summer-times gone by.

"While it is true that we help the farmer by destroying his insect pests, yet, let us remember that where there are no farms there are few birds. We need the farmer quite as much as he needs us.

"There are members of our race who feed upon snakes, and Farmer Brown has allowed them to indulge their peculiar tastes, although the snakes themselves are useful to him, as they, too, destroy his enemies, the insects. He has ever treated us with special favour and kindness.

"My feathered friends, for reasons of his own, the farmer requested and commanded our flocks to eat no cherries when they should become ripe, and to keep out of the corn-field at all times. Owning the land, he had a right to do so, and to punish all who disobeyed him. If the good farmer knew of the help we render in protecting his grain from the ravages of insects, I am sure he would gladly share with us his cherries, at least.

"Jim Crow and the Wren were trespassing when they perched on the corn-field fence, and should have heeded the warning of the Scare-

crow whom Farmer Brown placed in the field
to guard his property. The Scarecrow tells me
that he did his best to frighten the Crow away.
He waved his arms and shook his head; he
fluttered all the queer trimmings on his clothes,
and made frantic signals, but the Wren only
laughed, and the Crow looked scornful, though
I suppose he was quaking with fear all the
time.

"Doesn't the very fact that Farmer Brown,
at his own expense, sent the Scarecrow into the
field to simply scare the birds away prove that
he is a tender-hearted man, unwilling to kill
even the birds whom he considers his enemies?

"We admit that Farmer Brown fired the gun,
as the witnesses for the other side have said.
It may be that he didn't know that the gun
was loaded; anyway, we insist that the death
of the Wren was due to an accident which
would not have happened if Jim Crow and
the Wren had obeyed the Scarecrow. Accord-
ing to his own testimony, Jim Crow, fully aware
that his friend was badly hurt, and not knowing
whether he would live or die, left him where he
had fallen. Birds of the jury, consider well before placing your confidence in the testimony

of a witness too cowardly to help a friend in trouble. Let me warn you to be careful about believing the stories of others, who, with base ingratitude toward the farmer, now speak ill of him."

The Sparrow Hawk grew eloquent in telling how Farmer Brown was loved and respected among his fellow men, and the trust and confidence every one seemed to feel in him.

"Birds of the ury, " said he, in closing, " man is, and has been, our powerful friend and advocate. He has chosen our unworthy comrades as subjects of immortal poems. He has been pleased to attribute to our race qualities we would do well to cultivate. He has caused beautiful paintings of our ancestors to adorn the walls of his home and public places. His noblest sons have devoted their lives to the study of ourselves and our customs. He has edited magazines in our behalf. In the schools he has established, his children are taught to love and respect us ; even his tiniest little ones delight in stories regarding our lives. He considers our citizens the most beautiful singers in the world, and has written volumes in praise of our simple music. He has organised societies

"THE FARMER . . . HEARD THE JOYOUS OUTBURST."

for our protection, and has passed the most
rigid laws for our preservation.

"Birds of the jury, I know whereof I speak ;
from one end of this broad land to the other
I have winged my way, and never in all my
experience have I met a representative of the
human race more worthy of respect and honour
than Farmer Brown, in whose name I plead and
ask for justice."

As the Sparrow Hawk closed, a chorus of
applause spread throughout the meadow.

The farmer, working in a distant field, heard
the joyous outburst and smiled. Though he
scarce knew why, he felt happier and glad
to be in the outdoor world with his friends, the
birds.

CHAPTER V.

The judge in his most solemn manner delivered his charge to the jury. He told them that a man who kills birds not only sins against the feathered tribe, but is guilty of interfering with the laws of nature; that only through the tireless work of the birds the insect hosts are kept from destroying everything that grows; that the death of any bird means an increase of the insects upon which it fed. If, in their judgment, Farmer Brown intentionally killed the Wren, their verdict must be "guilty;" if he did not, their verdict should be "not guilty."

In solemn state the jurors marched across the meadow to a distant corner, in charge of a silent Raven, who remained on guard.

Judge Hawk Owl, having a great appetite himself, sent a lunch to the jury in their corner. The Brown Thrashers, who furnished the lunch,

58

smiled as they read the following bill of fare,
written by the judge on a burdock-leaf.

<pre>
        Caterpillars   Earthworms
            Grasshoppers   Snails
        Spiders   Crickets
                Beetles   Ants
            Plant-lice   Gadflies
                    Cutworms
                    Bugs
Wasps   Weevils   Web-worms   Grubs   ·
    Katy-dids   Potato-bugs   Canker-worms
                    Flies
Ragweed Seeds   Thistle Seeds   Mustard Seeds
        Wild Fruits   Cherries   Apples
        Beechnuts   Mountain-ash Berries
                    Acorns   ·
</pre>

The worms, alive and squirming, were taste-
fully arranged on oak-leaves, and carried to the
birds in the bills of the waiters, who were English Sparrows. The hungry Robin on the jury,
forgetting his manners, ate all the mountain-
ash berries himself.

Whatever was the reason, the jurors quickly
decided on a verdict and were taken back to
court.

Not a sound was heard but the wind in the
grasses around them when the Pigeon, who was

clerk of the court, said, " What is your verdict, guilty, or not guilty ? "

The farmer, mending a fence near by, suddenly felt a strange stillness, and wondered at it ; then, to cheer his loneliness, he began to whistle. While he whistled, came the answer, " Guilty."

Then rose the judge and pronounced sentence.

" Farmer Brown has had a fair and just trial before a jury of our best citizens, and his defence has been conducted by one of our most famous birds. The jury has found him guilty of murder, and, whatever may be my feelings in the matter, I have but one duty to perform.

" If Farmer Brown should lose his sight, he could kill no more birds.

" It is the judgment of this court that, when the leaves on the maples begin to turn, all the Butcher-birds upon the farm shall agree upon a day and hour when it will be possible to find the farmer in a distant field far from home. Then with their strong bills they shall attack his eyes, nor cease from their efforts until he is quite blind.

" Sheriff, adjourn court."

The hollow voice ceased. Even the Blue Jay felt a thrill of horror as he listened. The Sparrow Hawk, in dismay, flew to the side of the English Sparrow for advice.

"Such an awful sentence!" he exclaimed. "Better be dead than blind! What can we do to save him? To carry out this sentence will bring upon our race the just indignation of all mankind. Surely it could not teach these farmers that we are their friends and helpers. It was wrong to give that Hawk Owl so much power. I have too much faith in the good-will of our race to believe that they approve of this terrible sentence, — why, it would be a crime! What can we do — what shall we do to save poor Farmer Brown?"

"Don't be so nervous, friend Hawk," said the city Sparrow, "we will appeal the case." With a proud sense of his importance, the tiny bird then told the Sparrow Hawk just what ought to be done.

At midnight, less than a week after the Sparrow Hawk announced that he would appeal from the decision of the meadow judge, he and the Blue Jay met in the august presence of Chief Justice Great Horned Owl and Associate Justices Barn Owl, Barred Owl, Acadian Owl, and Screech Owl, the Supreme Court of the Feathered Tribe.

It is one thing to meet an Owl in the bright sunshine, when he is dazed and helpless because of his dim sight, but to meet five Owls in the depths of the woods, at midnight, is quite different. No wonder that the two birds of the daytime were startled by every rustling leaf or creaking twig. In spite of his fear, the Sparrow Hawk made a noble appeal in behalf of the farmer, and the Blue Jay, in his terror, spoke with dreadful earnestness against him.

The judges meanwhile listened in solemn silence, their eyes gleaming in the darkness. Then spoke the Great Horned Owl: " Command the sheriff to appear before us at day-break. To him we will announce our decision. Now you may go."

Having done their duty, the two birds silently and swiftly made their escape, nor paused until the dense woods were far behind them.

In the early dawn the birds met for the last time in the meadow, to hear the message of the Raven. When they heard it, all but a few went quietly and sadly on their way. The Supreme

Court of the Feathered Tribe had decided against the farmer. "The judgment of the Hawk Owl is right," it declared.

In despair, the Sparrow Hawk again sought the advice of his little friend. "There is hope even now," said he, touched by the sad, drooping figure before him. "Come, cheer up!" he went on. "Do you know who is King of the Birds?"

"Why, the Eagle, of course," faltered the other.

"Well, then, my friend, go to the Eagle, and ask him to pardon your farmer. You are a bird of swift flight; go, then, and tell your story."

The Sparrow Hawk took courage. "My dear English Sparrow," said he, "I will go; if I fail to return with a pardon, before the maple-leaves are streaked with gold, you will never see me more."

"For the welfare of our race, I wish you success," replied the Sparrow, who wished the farmer punished in a way to teach the usefulness of birds, not their powers of vengeance.

On swift wing the Sparrow Hawk sped through the summer air, and the farmer, little dreaming the mission on which he went, watched him out of sight.

The Eagle was dining at Niagara Falls when the Sparrow Hawk found him. He listened attentively to the story of the trial of Farmer Brown. Little he cared about the death of the Wren, but it pleased him to be acknowledged King of the Birds, and the injustice of the sentence imposed by the Hawk Owl angered him.

The moments passed, yet the Eagle said not a word. The Sparrow Hawk, listening to the mournful roar of the falls in the distance, felt a strange, uneasy loneliness.

Finally the majestic Eagle spoke.

"Go back to your lowly comrades," said he, "and bid them know that I, King of the Birds, do banish them from the lands of Farmer Brown; while he lives shall they not return. Before the maple-leaves are gold and crimson, they must all be gone. Thus will man learn the value of birds."

The Sparrow Hawk, bowing low, thanked the Eagle for his mercy in sparing the farmer's sight; then, greatly wondering, he sped on his homeward way.

"HE LISTENED ATTENTIVELY TO THE STORY."

CHAPTER VI.

"CURIOUS where the birds are gone," re-
marked Farmer Brown, in the early autumn.
"I never knew them to disappear so suddenly
before, and all at the same time, too. Why, the
Robins sometimes stay until much later than
this. Must be we are going to have an early
winter, and the birds knew it by instinct.
Curious, though."

Through the long months that followed, not
a winter bird visited the farm. The Chick-
adees, Nuthatches, Brown Creepers, and Woodpeckers passed it by, and the bunches of eggs
hidden in the bark of trees and in fences were
left to hatch into millions of insects and worms
when the first warm days of spring came.

Jim Crow, the rascal, watched the farm as
well as he could from a distance. Flying low
across the fields, and calling, "Caw — caw —
caw," as loud and saucily as he could, became

his favourite amusement. Of course he was
careful not to alight anywhere on the farm,
and the birds could not accuse him of break-
ing the law.

"Farmer Brown," said the rogue to himself,
"doesn't know how fond I am of him ; why, he
ate up his strongest witness when he dined on
that Brown Turkey! My! what if that Turkey had been spared to testify at the trial. It
would have been 'good-bye' to you, Jim."

"What makes you hang around the old
farm all the time, Jim?" asked the Blue Jay,
one day.

"I'm homesick," answered the Crow, solemnly.

"Oh, you tender-hearted birdie," laughed
the Blue Jay. "You're just the sort of a gentleman to be sentimental. Seriously, though,"
he added, "most of the birds do miss their old
homes, and would go back if they could; they
say they can't settle down and be as contented
anywhere else."

"That's just my case," agreed the Crow,
"I'm so homesick."

"How is Farmer Brown getting along without the birds?" inquired the Blue Jay, regard-

less of the Crow's pretended sadness. "Is he as good-natured as he used to be?"

"Well," slowly answered the Crow, "as far as I can see, he appears to be an even-tempered man these days, — mad all the time."

"Isn't the farm prospering?" persisted the Blue Jay.

"The bugs and worms are prospering," replied the Crow. "They have eaten everything green on the place, and I guess they have tasted of Farmer Brown, if his actions are to be trusted. Harvest-time won't mean anything to him this year; the boys won't steal his pumpkins to make Jack-o'-lanterns of, that's sure"

"The very horses were so tormented by the gadflies and other insects that they ran away, — even old Dan went with the rest of them. What happened to the cows I don't know, but the pigs trotted to market, and asked the butcher to make them into sausages, if he would be so kind."

"Hold on, Jim," protested the Blue Jay, "I've been something of a story-teller myself, but — "

"You shouldn't interrupt the speaker," ob-

jected the Crow. "Mrs. Brown went away
long ago. One day when she was outdoors,
holding up her dress to keep clear of the
worms and snakes, and walking carefully, like
this," he mimicked, "I heard her say she
wouldn't live another day in a house where
crickets and grasshoppers danced on the din-
ing-table, and the spiders were crawling everywhere.

"The hired man has gone, too, — said no
money would tempt him to stay where he
found snakes in his boots, and hornets in his
hat. Tramps don't come within a mile of the
place.

"Of course you enjoy a joke as well as I do,
and you would laugh if you could see that poor
old farmer, trying new insect powders all the
time, and working from daylight till dark to get
rid of the pests. He's getting discouraged,
though, and it's lucky for him that this farm
isn't all he owns in the world."

After one more season, Jim Crow lost his
interest in the desolate, abandoned farm. There
was no one left whom he could tease when
Farmer Brown locked the door of the dreary
farmhouse, and returned no more.

Many happy years passed away before the good man died, and the birds sang above his grave.

When that time came, the Eagle sent his messengers, the white-winged Gulls, to tell the birds who belonged on the farm to return to their old home.

From the north, the east, the south, and the west came generations of birds who claimed the farm as the home of their ancestors, and among the first to arrive was Jim Crow, — old, to be sure, but as droll a scamp as ever.

The son of Farmer Brown, who inherited the place, encouraged by the return of the birds, moved back to the home of his childhood, and with a resolute heart made a renewed attempt to reclaim the land. He was more successful than he had dared to dream, and, in his gratitude to his tiny helpers in feathers, he planted wild fruit-trees and mulberry-bushes for them by the roadside, and protected them in every way in his power, so that the old farm became a paradise for birds.

Every morning a chorus of thanksgiving rose from the orchard and fields, and at twilight the evening hymn of the birds floated out upon the

summer air like a benediction at the close of
day.

Jim Crow, no longer afraid of guns, became
quite domestic in his tastes, and the Blue Jay,
who had vainly searched the favourite haunts of
his old-time friend, found him, at last, eating
corn with the barn-yard fowls.

"You see," explained Jim Crow, "I thought
I had better settle down and be one of the
family, it will make it so much easier for me
to keep track of the Turkeys' eggs."

A Song of Thanksgiving

COSY CORNER SERIES

It is the intention of the publishers that this series shall contain only the very highest and purest literature, — stories that shall not only appeal to the children themselves, but be appreciated by all those who feel with them in their joys and sorrows, — stories that shall be most particularly adapted for reading aloud in the family circle.

The numerous illustrations in each book are by well-known artists, and each volume has a separate attractive cover design.

Each, 1 vol., 16mo, cloth $0.50

By ANNIE FELLOWS JOHNSTON

The Little Colonel.

The scene of this story is laid in Kentucky. Its heroine is a small girl, who is known as the Little Colonel, on account of her fancied resemblance to an old-school Southern gentleman, whose fine estate and old family are famous in the region. This old Colonel proves to be the grandfather of the child.

The Giant Scissors.

This is the story of Joyce and of her adventures in France, — the wonderful house with the gate of The Giant Scissors, Jules, her little playmate, Sister Denisa, the cruel Brossard, and her dear Aunt Kate. Joyce is a great friend of the Little Colonel, and in later volumes shares with her the delightful experiences of the " House Party " and the " Holidays."

By ANNIE FELLOWS JOHNSTON (Continued)

Two Little Knights of Kentucky,

WHO WERE THE LITTLE COLONEL'S NEIGHBORS.

In this volume the Little Colonel returns to us like an old friend, but with added grace and charm. She is not, however, the central figure of the story, that place being taken by the " two little knights."

Cicely and Other Stories for Girls.

The readers of Mrs. Johnston's charming juveniles will be glad to learn of the issue of this volume for young people, written in the author's sympathetic and entertaining manner.

Aunt 'Liza's Hero and Other Stories.

A collection of six bright little stories, which will appeal to all boys and most girls.

Big Brother.

A story of two boys. The devotion and care of Steven, himself a small boy, for his baby brother, is the theme of the simple tale, the pathos and beauty of which has appealed to so many thousands.

Ole Mammy's Torment.

" Ole Mammy's Torment " has been fitly called " a classic of Southern life." It relates the haps and mishaps of a small negro lad, and tells how he was led by love and kindness to a knowledge of the right.

The Story of Dago.

In this story Mrs. Johnston relates the story of Dago, a pet monkey, owned jointly by two brothers. Dago tells his own story, and the account of his haps and mishaps is both interesting and amusing.

By EDITH ROBINSON

A Little Puritan's First Christmas.

A story of Colonial times in Boston, telling how Christmas was invented by Betty Sewall, a typical child of the Puritans, aided by her brother Sam.

A Little Daughter of Liberty.

The author's motive for this story is well indicated by a quotation from her introduction, as follows :

" One ride is memorable in the early history of the American Revolution, the well-known ride of Paul Revere. Equally deserving of commendation is another ride, — untold in verse or story, its records preserved only in family papers or shadowy legend, the ride of Anthony Severn was no less historic in its action or memorable in its consequences."

A Loyal Little Maid.

A delightful and interesting story of Revolutionary days, in which the child heroine, Betsey Schuyler, renders important services to George Washington.

A Little Puritan Rebel.

Like Miss Robinson's successful story of " A Loyal Little Maid," this is another historical tale of a real girl, during the time when the gallant Sir Harry Vane was governor of Massachusetts.

A Little Puritan Pioneer.

The scene of this story is laid in the Puritan settlement at Charlestown. The little girl heroine adds another to the list of favorites so well known to the young people.   .

A Little Puritan Bound Girl.

A story of Boston in Puritan days, which is of great interest to youthful readers.

By OUIDA (Louise de la Ramée)

A Dog of Flanders : A Christmas Story.
Too well and favorably known to require description.

The Nürnberg Stove.
This beautiful story has never before been published at a popular price.

A Provence Rose.
A story perfect in sweetness and in grace.

Findelkind.
A charming story about a little Swiss herdsman.

By MISS MULOCK

The Little Lame Prince.
A delightful story of a little boy who has many adventures by means of the magic gifts of his fairy godmother.

Adventures of a Brownie.
The story of a household elf who torments the cook and gardener, but is a constant joy and delight to the children who love and trust him.

His Little Mother.
Miss Mulock's short stories for children are a constant source of delight to them, and " His Little Mother," in this new and attractive dress, will be welcomed by hosts of youthful readers.

Little Sunshine's Holiday.
An attractive story of a summer outing. " Little Sunshine " is another of those beautiful child-characters for which Miss Mulock is so justly famous.

By *JULIANA HORATIA EWING*

Jackanapes.
A new edition, with new illustrations, of this exquisite and touching story, dear alike to young and old.

Story of a Short Life.
This beautiful and pathetic story will never grow old. It is a part of the world's literature, and will never die.

A Great Emergency.
How a family of children prepared for a great emergency, and how they acted when the emergency came.

The Trinity Flower.
In this little volume are collected three of Mrs. Ewing's best short stories for the young people.

Madam Liberality.
From her cradle up Madam Liberality found her chief delight in giving.

By *FRANCES MARGARET FOX*

The Little Giant's Neighbours.
A charming nature story of a "little giant" whose neighbours were the creatures of the field and garden.

Farmer Brown and the Birds.
A little story which teaches children that the birds are man's best friends.

Betty of Old Mackinaw.
A charming story of child-life, appealing especially to the little readers who like stories of "real people."

Mother Nature's Little Ones.
Curious little sketches describing the early lifetime, or "childhood," of the little creatures out-of-doors.

By WILL ALLEN DROMGOOLE

The Farrier's Dog and His Fellow.

This story, written by the gifted young Southern woman, will appeal to all that is best in the natures of the many admirers of her graceful and piquant style.

The Fortunes of the Fellow.

Those who read and enjoyed the pathos and charm of " The Farrier's Dog and His Fellow " will welcome the further account of the " Adventures of Baydaw and the Fellow " at the home of the kindly smith among the Green Hills of Tennessee.

By FRANCES HODGES WHITE

Helena's Wonderworld.

A delightful tale of the adventures of a little girl in the mysterious regions beneath the sea.

Aunt Nabby's Children.

This pretty little story, touched with the simple humo of country life, tells of two children, who, adopted by Aunt Nabby, have also won their way into the affections of the village squire.

By CHARLES LEE SLEIGHT

The Prince of the Pin Elves.

A fascinating story of the underground adventures of a sturdy, reliant American boy among the elves and gnomes.

The Water People.

A companion volume and in a way a sequel to " The Prince of the Pin Elves," relating the adventures of " Harry " among the " water people." While it has the same characters as the previous book, the story is complete in itself.

By OTHER AUTHORS

The Flight of Rosy Dawn. By PAULINE BRADFORD MACKIE.

The Christmas of little Wong Jan, or " Rosy Dawn," a young Celestial of San Francisco, is the theme of this pleasant little story.

Susanne. By FRANCES J. DELANO.

This little story will recall in sweetness and appealing charm the work of Kate Douglas Wiggin and Laura E. Richards.

Millicent in Dreamland. By EDNA S. BRAINERD.

The quaintness and fantastic character of Millicent's adventures in Dreamland have much of the fascination of " Alice in Wonderland," and all small readers of " Alice " will enjoy making Millicent's acquaintance.

Jerry's Reward. By EVELYN SNEAD BARNETT.

This is an interesting and wholesome little story of the change that came over the thoughtless imps on Jefferson Square when they learned to know the stout-hearted Jerry and his faithful Peggy.

A Bad Penny. By JOHN T. WHEELWRIGHT.

No boy should omit reading this vivid story of the New England of 1812.

Gatty and I. By FRANCES E. CROMPTON.

The small hero and heroine of this little story are twins, " strictly brought up." It is a sweet and wholesome little story.

Prince Yellowtop. By KATE WHITING PATCH.
A pretty little fairy tale.

The Little Christmas Shoe. By JANE P. SCOTT-WOODRUFF.
A touching story of Yule-tide.

The Little Professor. By IDA HORTON CASH.
A quaint tale of a quaint little girl.

The Seventh Daughter. By GRACE WICKHAM CURRAN.
One of the best stories for little girls that has been published for a long time.

The Making of Zimri Bunker: A TALE OF NANTUCKET. By W. J. LONG, Ph. D.
This is a charming story of Nantucket folk by a young clergyman who is already well known through his contributions to the *Youth's Companion, St. Nicholas*, and other well-known magazines. The story deals with a sturdy American fisher lad, during the war of 1812.

The King of the Golden River: A LEGEND OF STIRIA. By JOHN RUSKIN.
Written fifty years or more ago, and not originally intended for publication, this little fairy tale soon became known and made a place for itself.

Little Peterkin Vandike. By CHARLES STUART PRATT.
The author's dedication furnishes a key to this charming story :

" I dedicate this book, made for the amusement (and perchance instruction) of the boys who may read it, to the memory of one boy, who would have enjoyed as much as Peterkin the plays of the Poetry Party, but who has now marched out of the ranks of boyhood."

CPSIA information can be obtained
at www.ICGtesting.com
Printed in the USA
BVHW031628211119
564443BV00004B/189/P